Georgia, My State
Habitats

Coast

by Doraine Bennett

STATE
STANDARDS
PUBLISHING

Your State • Your Standards • Your Grade Level

Dear Educators, Librarians and Parents . . .

Thank you for choosing the *"Georgia, My State"* Series! We have designed this series to support the Georgia Department of Education's Georgia Performance Standards for elementary level Georgia studies. Each book in the series has been written at appropriate grade level as measured by the ATOS Readability Formula for Books (Accelerated Reader), the Lexile Framework for Reading, and the Fountas & Pinnell Benchmark Assessment System for Guided Reading. Photographs and/or illustrations, captions, and other design elements have been included to provide supportive visual messaging to enhance text comprehension. Glossary and Word Index sections introduce key new words and help young readers develop skills in locating and combining information.

We wish you all success in using the *"Georgia, My State"* Series to meet your student or child's learning needs. For additional sources of information, see www.georgiaencyclopedia.org.

Jill Ward, President

Publisher
State Standards Publishing, LLC
1788 Quail Hollow
Hamilton, GA 31811
USA
1.866.740.3056
www.statestandardspublishing.com

Library of Congress Cataloging-in-Publication Data
Bennett, Doraine, 1953-
  Coast / by Doraine Bennett.
      p. cm. -- (Georgia, my state. Habitats)
  Includes index.
  ISBN-13: 978-1-935077-35-0 (hardcover)
  ISBN-10: 1-935077-35-X (hardcover)
  ISBN-13: 978-1-935077-40-4 (pbk.)
  ISBN-10: 1-935077-40-6 (pbk.)
  1. Coastal ecology--Georgia--Juvenile literature. 2. Estuaries--Georgia--Juvenile literature.
I. Title.
  QH105.G4B46 2009
  577.5'109758--dc22
                                    2009012442

Table of Contents

Cannonball Jellyfish

Least Terns

Sanderlings

Mountains

Piedmont

Coastal Plain

Marsh and Swamp

← Coast

Atlantic Ocean

A coast is the place where the ocean meets the land.

What is a Coast?

Waves lap against the sand on Cumberland Island. A cannonball jellyfish lies stranded on the beach. Sanderlings skitter along the edge of the water looking for food. A least tern feeds her chick. This is Georgia's Coast **habitat**. A habitat is a place where plants and animals live.

The Atlantic Ocean first meets land in Georgia at the **Barrier Islands**. They protect the mainland of Georgia from the wind and waves.

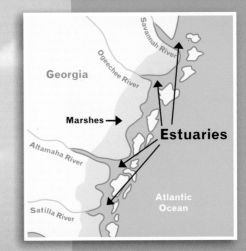

Estuaries form where fresh water from creeks and rivers meets salt water from the ocean.

Marshes separate the Barrier Islands from the mainland of Georgia.

What are Marshes and Estuaries?

The ocean water flows around the Barrier Islands. It mixes with fresh water to form **estuaries**. An estuary is the place where fresh water from rivers and creeks meets salt water from the ocean. Salt water marshes lie further inland. Marsh land is low and covered in water all or most of the time. Estuaries and **salt marshes** separate the Barrier Islands from Georgia's mainland.

The salt marshes and estuaries are **nurseries**! They protect many animals while they grow. Blue crabs, fish, and shrimp come here from the ocean after they are born. When they are young adults, they swim back. Without the salt marshes and estuaries, we wouldn't have seafood to eat!

Sea Oats

Morning Glory and Grasses

Powerful waves sometimes cause erosion on the beach.

Woody plants grow on older dunes further inland.

Sand dunes form near the shore.

8

Let's Go to the Beach!

Georgia's beaches are on the ocean side of the Barrier Islands. Piles of sand called **dunes** form near the shore. The dunes store up sand. When storms come, powerful waves wear away the coast. This process is called **erosion**. Sand from the dunes replaces the sand lost from the beach.

Sea oats grow on the dunes. They grow fast and tall. They help to keep the dunes stable. Morning glories and grasses grow on the dunes, too. They help keep the sand in place. Woody plants grow on older dunes further inland.

It's a Fact!

Keep off the dunes! Signs like these ask people to stay off the dunes. Walking on the dunes causes the sand to erode.

Seagulls

Willet

Pelican

Clam

American oystercatchers pull clam shells apart with their powerful bills.

Birds in the Air and on the Water

The beach is a noisy place! Water birds chatter and screech. Their bills and legs help them catch food. Willets use their long pointed bills to find food in the sand. Pelicans use their long legs to wade into the water. They scoop up fish with their big bills.

This black skimmer is looking for fish to eat.

Seagulls soar overhead looking for food. They eat fish. They will also eat bread and other food that people throw in the air. American oystercatchers search the shoreline for oysters and clams to eat. They pull the shells open with their powerful bills. Skimmers fly low over the water looking for fish.

Camouflage makes the ghost crab hard to see.

Clams burrow into the sand.

Horseshoe crabs are not crabs at all!

Sand Dollar

Shells and sand dollars wash up on the beach.

Animals on the Beach

The sun beats down on the beach. Sometimes the sand gets too hot to walk on. How do animals survive here? Crabs, clams, and worms **burrow** into the sand. They dig holes. The burrows keep them cool and safe.

Ghost crabs live on the beach. They can run sideways, forward, and backward. They can run as fast as 10 miles per hour! The ghost crab is almost the same color as the sand. This **camouflage** makes the crab hard to see.

Shells and sand dollars wash up on the beach. Horseshoe crabs sometimes swim near the shore. They are not crabs at all!

It's a Fact!

Ghost crabs burrow into the sand. In winter, they **hibernate** in their burrows. They sleep for six weeks. Most animals that hibernate store fat to survive. The ghost crab stores oxygen in its gills to breathe under the ground.

13

The turtle digs a hole to lay her eggs and covers them with sand.

Turtle Hatchlings

DO NOT DISTURB
SEA TURTLE NEST
VIOLATORS SUBJECT TO FINES AND IMPRISONMENT

A loggerhead turtle comes ashore to lay her eggs.

Don't Touch Those Eggs!

It's nighttime on the beach. A female sea turtle comes ashore to lay her eggs. She drags her heavy body across the beach with her flippers. It's slow going!

She digs a deep hole with her back flippers. She lays about 120 eggs in the hole. She covers the eggs with sand. Then she slowly crawls back to the ocean. The baby sea turtles are on their own! Soon, the eggs hatch. The turtles are born. The baby sea turtle **hatchlings** head for the ocean.

Many sea turtles don't survive. Raccoons, foxes, and other animals eat the eggs. Crabs and seagulls eat the hatchlings. Humans disturb nests and take the eggs. Now, it is illegal to touch sea turtles, their eggs, or the hatchlings.

Painted Bunting

Live Oaks and Saw Palmettos

Deer

Magnolia

Spanish Moss

Many trees near the coast are draped with Spanish moss.

Forests on the Beach?

At the center of the Barrier Islands are **maritime forests**. Maritime forests grow near the ocean. Live oaks and other trees are draped with Spanish moss. Spanish moss is an **epiphyte**. It gets food and water from the air and rain. Magnolias and cabbage palms grow here. Songbirds like the painted bunting nest in their branches.

Muscadine vines grow in the trees. They block the sun and make the forest dark. Saw palmettos carpet the forest floor. Deer, turkey, and squirrels live in the forests. Black racers hide in the trees and bushes.

It's a Fact!

The southern black racer moves very fast. It can climb and swim, too. It uses **mimicry** to defend itself. It makes a rattling sound by vibrating its tail in dry leaves or grass. Predators may think it is a poisonous rattlesnake and leave it alone. But black racers are not poisonous. They are helpful to people. They eat rats and insect pests.

Bullfrogs need fresh water to survive.

Otters play in the sloughs.

Wild horses head to the sloughs when they get thirsty.

A yellow-crowned night heron wades in for a drink.

Freshwater sloughs in the forests catch rainwater.

Come Take a Drink!

There are small ponds in the maritime forest called **freshwater sloughs**. They hold rainwater. Birds and animals come here to drink. Frogs and turtles live near the water. Minks and otters play here.

Alligators do not like salt water. They gather around the sloughs. Wild horses roam some of the Barrier Islands. They usually travel in herds, or groups. They come to the freshwater sloughs to drink, too. These horses are not true wild horses. They are **descendants** of horses that strayed or ran away from their owners. Descendants are children and grandchildren of people or animals.

Alligators

Some people live on the Georgia coast.

Many people come for a visit.

People Live Here, Too

Animals and birds aren't the only ones who live on the Georgia coast. People live on some of the Barrier Islands, too! Others come to swim in the ocean and enjoy the warm sunshine. They come to ride motor boats and sailboats. They come to see the birds and animals. They also come here to catch fish!

Most people come to four of the Barrier Islands. They come to Jekyll Island and St. Simons Island. They also come to Sea Island and Tybee Island. Can you guess why?

Glossary

Barrier Islands – Islands that protect the mainland from the wind and waves of the ocean.

burrow – A hole that an animal digs in the ground for protection.

camouflage – A way animals hide by looking like their surroundings.

descendants – Children and grandchildren of people or animals.

dunes – Piles of sand that form near the shore of an ocean.

epiphyte – A plant that gets food and water from the air and rain.

erosion – Sand or soil being worn away by wind and water.

estuaries – Bodies of water where fresh water from rivers and creeks mixes with salt water from the ocean.

freshwater sloughs – Ponds on islands that hold fresh rainwater.

habitat – A place where plants and animals live.

hatchlings – Baby animals that are born by hatching from eggs.

hibernate – To sleep during the winter season, when food is scarce.

maritime forests – Forests that grow on barrier islands.

mimicry – A way some animals protect themselves by imitating animals that are harmful.

nurseries – Places that protect young animals or plants while they grow.

salt marshes – Land that is covered with salt water all or most of the time.

Word Index

Image Credits

About the Author

Doraine Bennett has a degree in professional writing from Columbus State University in Columbus, Georgia, and has been writing and teaching writing for over twenty years. She has authored numerous articles in magazines for both children and adults and is the editor of the National Infantry Association's *Infantry Bugler* magazine. Doraine enjoys reading and writing books and articles for children. She lives in Georgia with her husband, Cliff.